Romans

At His Feet Studies

By Hope A. Blanton and Christine B. Gordon

2nd Edition

To the amazing and gracious women at Redeemer Presbyterian Church in Lincoln, Nebraska:

Over ten years ago, you trusted us enough to join us on a journey through the Book of Romans, which has led to so much more.

Contents

How to Use This Study

There is no right way to lead a Bible study. Every Bible study group is made up of different types of people with various needs and dynamics. These are some suggestions that might be helpful when using At His Feet Studies. Read it through. Use what you want. Forget the rest. We're glad you're here.

A different approach to a familiar method

As with many Bible studies you're familiar with, we follow a pattern of observation, interpretation, and application, but the presentation may be a little different than what you're used to. Instead of bouncing between those three tasks, we group them.

First, you will read a biblical passage, and using the Observation Questions, you'll note the people mentioned, terms used, commands given, actions taken, and so on. This is arguably the most important step, as the Word of God itself is powerful and active.

In the next section, you will interpret the biblical passage with help from seminary-trained Chris. The Interpretation section is written in the style of most commentaries, offering a verse-by-verse explanation of the biblical passage. This section is rooted in study of the original language and multiple sources, including commentaries, original language helps, sermons, theological treatises, and personal conversations with seminary professors.

Finally, you will apply the biblical text to your life, assisted by licensed therapist Hope and her heart-engaging Reflection Questions.

In this way, you will read, interpret, and then reflect on a larger passage as a whole, keeping the words and message in their context.

What do I do each day?

You can read through and complete the entire study in one sitting or break it up. If you'd like to spread out your preparation a bit more, break it into three days: On day 1, read the biblical passage and complete the Observation Questions. On day 2, read the Interpretation section. On day 3, complete the Reflection Questions. You could even add a day 4 and attempt to memorize or simply meditate on the focus verse and/or write down your thoughts in the space for "Reflections, curiosities, frustrations."

How do I lead a group through this study?

It is always a good idea to read through the biblical passage out loud at the beginning of your time together. After reading the Scripture aloud, choose one or two Observation Questions and answer them as a group.

If most of your group has had a chance to read the Interpretation section on their own, ask them what stood out to them in that section and talk through parts of the commentary they may have highlighted. If you are leading a group with participants who have not had the time to read through the Interpretation section on their own, take the time to read it out loud as a group before asking this question.

Next, choose three or four of your favorite Reflection Questions and allow time for everyone who would like to offer their answers. These questions are written with the aim of both engaging your own heart and also engaging one another's hearts as you study together.

If you have the time, do all of the above *and* walk through all of the Reflection Questions. If you'd like, you could ask the group what questions or frustrations arose during their study.

Want an extra challenge?

Issue the challenge to your group to memorize the focus verse and say it together when you reconvene.

Questions? Reach out!

We would love to hear from you. Write us at athisfeetstudies@gmail.com.

The History Behind the Pages of Romans

"This letter is truly the most important piece in the New Testament. It is purest Gospel. It is well worth a Christian's while not only to memorize it word for word but also to occupy himself with it daily, as though it were the daily bread of the soul. It is impossible to read or to meditate on this letter too much or too well. The more one deals with it, the more precious it becomes and the better it tastes." So wrote Martin Luther, giant figure of the Reformation, in his "Preface to the Epistle to the Romans."[1]

Romans can be intimidating upon first glance, with its long, dense sentences and multiple chapters referencing the history of Israel. But in this book is a rich meal. It answers basic questions of the Christian faith like, Who is a sinner? What does Jesus's death have to do with me? and Can I ever lose God's love? You'll also find beautiful descriptions of God's sovereignty, which is his control over all things. You'll find insights into our struggle against sin and where God is in that process with us. You'll see God's desire and ability to work for the good of his people. In other words, if we study this foundational book that sometimes can be confusing, we will gain a lavish understanding of the gospel of Jesus.

Historical Setting

Paul wrote Romans around 57 AD, during his third missionary journey. He was ultimately planning to go to Spain, and Rome was situated along his way.

He needed the Romans' fellowship, their help, their encouragement, and their financial support. Paul probably wrote this letter, or epistle, to prepare the Romans for his visit. Rome was a large, crowded city in the first century AD, with a population of about 1 million in an area less than ten square miles. (By comparison, the island of Manhattan, New York, has 1.6 million people and three times the space. Think of how crowded Manhattan is!) There were estimated to be between 40,000 and 50,000 Jews in the city at this time.

Though we don't know how the church in Rome began, it is probable that there were Jewish Romans who were present at Pentecost who heard the gospel in their own language and were converted to Christianity. They would have then returned to Rome and started gathering together, probably meeting in homes. These early Christians would have followed a lot of the same practices as those in Jewish synagogues (see Acts 2). In 49 AD, the Emperor Claudius kicked the Jews out of Rome, including the Jewish Christians who had established the first church there. The Gentile Christians who remained would have continued to meet and grow without Jewish input or influence on the church.

People who became new believers at the time would have been Gentiles as well, creating a mostly Gentile church. When Claudius died in 54 AD and the edict lapsed, Jewish Christians came back into the city of Rome. The church they found would have felt very foreign to them. The Old Testament law-observing Jewish Christians found much conflict with the Gentile Christians who lived free of the restrictions of Mosaic law. These were brothers and sisters in Christ for sure, but there would have been noticeable differences in how they lived out their faith.

Paul's letter would have arrived soon after Jews began filtering back into the city. Because of the makeup of the church there, he emphasized two main themes in his letter to the Romans: (1) the justification of sinners (making us right before God) by God's grace alone in Christ through faith alone, regardless of who we are or how we behave, and (2) a new definition of the people of God, no longer according to ethnicity but according to faith in Jesus, so that all believers are the children of Abraham regardless of ethnic origin or religious practice.

These two themes are just as relevant to us today as they were to the original hearers of this letter. We too must let our justification by grace alone through faith alone seep into our thoughts, hearts, and bones. We need this doctrine to remind us that it is Christ who justifies when we want to defend ourselves in front of others. We need it to declare to our souls that it is grace that saves us when we find once again that our good actions are just not enough. We also need a generous, God-sized definition of the people of God when we are tempted to think we're better than others in the church because of our worship traditions, our gender, or our cultural preferences. May you find, as Martin Luther did, that the more you know of Jesus's gospel in Romans, "the more precious it becomes and the better it tastes."

Study 1

Not Ashamed of the Gospel

Read Romans 1 and 2

Observation Questions

1. What are the two reasons that Paul gives for why he is not ashamed of the gospel (Romans 1:16–17)?

2. According to Romans 1:18–23, what has caused the wrath of God? What has resulted from this (Romans 1:24–32)?

3. In Romans 2:1–5, what argument is Paul making about passing judgement on someone else?

4. What things does Paul say about the law in Romans 2:12–24?

Interpretation

Romans 1:1–7. The Book of Romans contains some weighty themes, such as justification of sinners by God's grace and a redefinition of the people of God. We might be tempted to think of the writer as quite impressive—perhaps Paul was beyond temptation or lived a higher or more beautiful life than we, normal believers. On the contrary, as we will see, God chose a man whose struggles were not so different from our own to bring the truth of the gospel to the Roman church. Paul describes himself in verse 1 as a "servant" (*doulas*), which is better translated as "slave." If we are among those who are "called to belong to Jesus Christ" (verse 6), we are literally slaves of Jesus.

"The obedience of faith" in verse 5 is the response the gospel demands. This faith is not only an emotion but also a commitment of total submission. Some people today claim that Jesus is their Savior but not their Lord, but Paul would have said that distinction is nonsense because one must lead to the other. This obedience of faith is for the sake of Christ's "name," which means for the sake of his "character" or his "reputation." The highest of all motives—and Paul's motive here—is not a passion for the lost, concern for our children, justice for the weak and oppressed, nor love for the church. It is zeal for the glory and reputation of Jesus Christ.

Romans 1:8–15. When Paul writes, "I am under obligation"—which could also be translated as "I am a debtor"—he means that Jesus had entrusted him with the gospel for the Romans, both Jewish and Gentile. He owed this debt to them: to faithfully preach the good news. Therefore, he wanted to come and preach to those in Rome as well. It must have greatly encouraged other churches to think that in Rome—at the center of such a huge and powerful empire, in a city that brought awe to those on the outskirts of that empire—there were brothers and sisters who shared their faith.

Romans 1:16. There is no reason for Paul to speak of not being ashamed of the gospel unless at some point he had been tempted to be ashamed. Here is *the* great apostle, the author of much of the New Testament, battling the temptation to keep quiet or to be ashamed of the gospel. We are not alone when we struggle in the same way.

Romans 1:17. Here Paul begins to discuss the huge theological idea of righteousness. What is it? Righteousness, or blamelessness, is a divine quality that represents God's character. But it is also a divine gift. Our righteousness before God is something that has been given to us. It is *from* God, and we obtain it *through* faith. God, because of his great mercy and love for us, has taken the initiative to put us in right standing with himself, though that standing is undeserved. This is the gospel.

Romans 1:18–20. Paul makes a sudden pivot after mentioning faith and begins a three-chapter-long explanation of why, without God's intervention, all people everywhere are condemned. Why? Paul names our biggest problem: a lack of righteousness. He pounds and pounds at the bad news of our sin in order to set us up for the good news of the gospel. The "wrath" of God in verse 18 is not primarily an emotion but an action, a judgement of sin. It is not like human anger, which is often an irrational, uncontrollable emotion laced with selfishness and a desire for revenge. Instead, God's anger is pure, holy, and directed at sin, which is totally offensive to him and damaging to us.

It can be difficult for us to understand wrath in the context of God's love. But remember, God's patience is extreme. When God descended to meet Moses on the mountain and passed before him, he revealed his character with these words, "The Lord, the Lord, a God merciful and gracious, slow to anger, and abounding in steadfast love and faithfulness" (Exodus 34:6). Isaiah speaks of God executing his wrath as a "strange deed" (Isaiah 28:21), something that he does slowly and reluctantly. Wrath is not where God begins; rather, it is the backdrop for his more regular work of mercy. God's wrath is an appropriate response to the wickedness of humanity. God has made his existence knowable through creation, so that godlessness is without excuse.

Romans 1:21–32. Paul is referring in these verses to God's created order, the way things were made to work. When we worship anything or anyone other than God, darkness and foolishness follow. Read verses 24, 26, and 28 together and hear the repetition of the phrase "God gave them up." This is God's judgement: to stop restraining our hearts from evil, to stop wooing us, and to give us over to the evil we pursue. We may think God's punishment looks like him actively making something bad happen to us or withholding some good from us. Paul's words tell us something different. His judgement looks like letting us go, giving us what we think we want. We do not naturally desire only good things. In fact, this passage paints a picture of God holding us back from the lusts of our hearts (verse 24), our dishonorable passions (verse 26), our debased minds (verse 28). When we're turned over to our sinful impulses and act on them, we damage our relationships with ourselves, others, and God.

Romans 2:1–5. Paul now begins arguing with an imaginary debate partner. He will continue this debate all the way through chapter 15, building his case and answering the objections of his invented questioner. In chapter 1, Paul described the open wickedness of the pagan Gentiles (non-Jews) that led to God's wrath. Here in chapter 2, he turns his attention to those who may think they're "better" than those with the terrible behavior described in chapter 1. This is the common human error of hypocrisy. We are critical of everyone else and lenient toward ourselves.

The word translated "forbearance" (or sometimes "tolerance") in verse 4 has the idea of the restraint of wrath. And "patience" refers to God's tolerance of our failures. We get a picture of the Almighty in his perfect holiness, holding back his absolutely justified punishment, all the while watching and giving us one opportunity after another after another to turn away from the sin we flirt with. This is not God giving us an excuse to sin; instead, by his kindness, he is leading us to repentance.

Romans 2:6–11. At first glance it may seem like Paul is contradicting everything he writes about the gospel in other places. If we are saved by faith, why does Paul emphasize our works? Though it is true that we are justified by faith in Christ alone, whether or not that faith exists can only be known by our works. James 2 tells us to show our faith, not by a profession of faith, but by our works. Jesus tells us in Matthew 7 that we will know the difference between false and real prophets by their fruits. Paul is not contradicting his words about the gospel but telling us that God expects our faith to be lived out in our actions.

Remember the context: Paul is addressing both upstanding Gentiles who believed in some sort of standards and stubborn, proud, arrogant Jews of his day who thought their position as chosen people of God, their possession of God's law, and their mark of circumcision could make them immune to God's wrath. But Paul shatters this illusion for both groups when he tells them in verse 6, "He will render to each one according to his works." It is not the possession of God's Word but obedience to it that marks a person as God's.

Romans 2:12–16. Paul is speaking in verse 12 of the amount of revelation given to Jews versus Gentiles of his day. God will judge people for the light they have been given. They will not be punished for revelation to which they did not have access. Because all humans are made in God's image, the basic requirements of the law are stamped on all human hearts. Paul continues his point here that none of us is righteous. The Jews had the law and did not obey it. The Gentiles had been given a conscience that acted for them as the law did for the Jews. They also did not obey this God-given guide. And so, though different in the amount of revelation they had been given, neither obeyed, both sinned, and all were condemned. Notice in verse 16 that judgement is a part of the gospel. The gospel is cheapened when we see it as only a relief from fear, loneliness, and other felt needs; it is no less than a rescue from the coming wrath.

Romans 2:17–29. During the Exile to Babylon (see 1 Chronicles 9:1), when Jerusalem was destroyed and God's people were scattered, Gentiles were said to speak badly about the Jewish God, saying that he was powerless to help his people. Now, in the Roman church, the hypocritical behavior of the Jews was once again causing the Gentiles to misunderstand who God really was. As an example, the ritual of circumcision was a sign that pointed to membership in the covenant God had made with his people, but most Jews misunderstood God's intention for circumcision, believing it to be what actually saved them and then acting in ways that contradicted it. At the same time, they judged the Gentiles who were not circumcised. Circumcision of the heart is needed, Paul says, not circumcision of the body. What saves is not a cutting off of flesh but an inward work of the Holy Spirit. For Christians, it is not baptism or even membership in the church that saves us, though these important signs point to the work of the Holy Spirit. It is always the state of the heart that matters.

Paul has begun in these first two chapters his masterful argument about righteousness and all humans' lack of it. Neither Jewish tradition nor good works nor membership in a religious community can make us good enough for God. The Holy God of Israel and all nations is perfectly righteous and therefore demands perfect righteousness. By giving us Jesus Christ, God has given that righteousness to us. What we deserve from God is his never-ending wrath, but what we are given is his lavish mercy. We, like our brothers and sisters in the Roman church, must look to God to make us right before him.

Reflection Questions

5. Often it is easy to idealize biblical writers, such as Paul, and assume they do not struggle with the same heart issues that we do. How does the idea that Paul might have been ashamed of the gospel change your perception of him? What part of the gospel have you struggled with being ashamed of?

6. Paul names our biggest problem as humans as a lack of righteousness. Without God's intervention all people, not just some, will be condemned. Do you view this as our biggest problem? Why or why not?

7. How have you always viewed God's wrath? How has this passage in Romans and interpretation in this study shifted your view?

8. God's judgement is to stop restraining our hearts from evil, giving us over to the evil we pursue. Does this description of God's judgement surprise you? How have you seen this play out in your life and the lives of those around you?

9. The Jews trusted in circumcision and in being the chosen people of God instead of in God himself for their salvation. What is the one thing that you tend to trust in for your salvation as much as or more than Jesus?

Focus verse

For I am not ashamed of the gospel, for it is the power of God for salvation to everyone who believes, to the Jew first and also to the Greek. For in it the righteousness of God is revealed from faith to faith, as it is written, "The righteous shall live by faith."

Romans 1:16–17

Reflections, curiosities, frustrations:

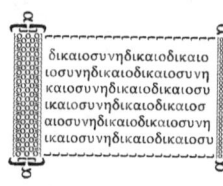

Study 2

None Is Righteous, No, Not One

Read Romans 3 and 4

Observation Questions

1. According to Romans 3:9–20, who is found righteous? What are some statements made about humans in these verses?

2. What statements does Paul make about faith in Romans 3:21–31? What is Paul's bottom line in regards to faith, Jews, and Gentiles according to Romans 3:30?

3. What is the relationship between circumcision and righteousness (Romans 4:1–12)?

4. According to Romans 4:13–23, what promise was given to Abraham, and how is it connected to faith?

Interpretation

Paul continues his reasoning with his imaginary opponent. The opponent is pulling out every argument they can to disagree with Paul and prove they shouldn't be judged. Paul won't back down.

Romans 3:1–4. In response to the first argument—that perhaps the unfaithfulness of the chosen people meant that God himself had been unfaithful—Paul unleashes the first use of his phrase "not at all," which could be translated something like "not on your life" or "not in a thousand years."

Romans 3:5–8. Paul's imaginary rival offers two more useless arguments: First, if God gets more glory when we sin, shouldn't he let us out of being punished for it? Why punish someone for giving God glory? Paul tells us he is using a human analogy to make a point that is ridiculous—God is not a cruel master who creates humans only to damn them.

Secondly, the antagonist says, Why not sin so that good may come out of it? Don't the ends (God's glory) justify the means (me sinning)? Aren't I doing God a favor? Paul doesn't even take the time to answer that one.

Romans 3:9–18. In a classic rabbinical move of putting together passages like a string of pearls, Paul sums up his long argument with verses from the Old Testament. He quotes from Psalm 14:1–3, 5:9, 10:7, and 36:1 and Isaiah 59:7–8 to picture sin as a cruel dictator who holds the human race, even Jews with all of their privileges, as prisoners of guilt and under judgement.

First, in verses 10–12, we read about the rebellion of sin. Not only do we disobey, but we actually turn away from our creator. Next, in verses 13–16, we see the pervasiveness of sin. We are both sinners and saints. This is where reformed people glean the doctrine of total depravity. It is not that we are as corrupt and wicked as we could possibly be; rather, it is that every part of us has been corrupted or is broken. Notice all the references to parts of our being: throats, tongues, lips, mouths, feet. Yes, we are created in God's image and are therefore inherently good and full of dignity. And also, our minds and bodies have been affected by sin. Finally, in verses 17–18, we understand that sin is universal. The root of our difficulty is that we do not fear God.

Romans 3:19–20. This is Paul's ultimate goal in his long argument: "so that every mouth may be stopped." We must shut our mouths instead of making excuses for our sin and trying to escape God's judgement.

Romans 3:21. Paul has spent two chapters explaining that no one is good enough for God. But in verse 21, we find the hope of the gospel breaking through. It is God who makes us good enough. The word translated "righteousness" here is the Greek word *dikaiosunē,* which Paul uses throughout this passage to mean both "righteous" and "justified." To be justified is to be declared or made righteous. Think of it as a verb: God has "righteous-ed" us. He has made us acceptable, good, and upright in God's sight.

Romans 3:22–24. All humans fail to live up to God's image in which we were made. The righteousness Paul describes comes by God's grace, as a gift from him, and not from the law. This must have sounded like crazy talk to the Jews, who held the law in such esteem. We believers may not rely on our keeping of the Mosaic law, but we may think it is our good morals or daily religiosity that makes us righteous before God. Paul would say to us what he said to the Romans: You are made right with God by God, as a gift from him.

Romans 3:25. The term *propitiation* means "to calm, appease, or satisfy." Perhaps it is unsettling to know that God's wrath—his righteous anger toward sin—must be appeased to bring peace between God and sinners. God took the initiative and directed the wrath our sin deserved on his Son, Jesus. In his patient self-control and restraint, God left the sins of generations past unpunished for a season until in the fullness of time he could punish these sins by Christ's death.

Romans 3:26–31. In chapter 2, Paul told us that our works, which reveal our faith or lack thereof, will be judged. Is he saying now that works don't matter? Paul is saying that we are made righteous with God, or justified, not by works but by our faith. That is, we're not saved by our works, but they are evidence of our *faith*, which is given by God to both Jews and Gentiles.

Romans 4. Is this a new religion? It would have felt that way to Jews who knew only the dutiful practice of the law. But Paul begins to paint for them a different picture—not a religion at all, as far as ceremonies and rules go, but a walk of faith. Far from being new, it is the flowering of a seed whose roots go all the way back to Abraham, the respected and righteous father of Judaism, and of all believers.

Romans 4:1–3. It makes sense that Paul would use Abraham as an example. Abraham was, of course, understood by Paul's Jewish readers to be righteous. But most would have said that Abraham was righteous because of his good works, or even because of his faithfulness. Here they misunderstood Abraham's relationship with God.

Consider the context of the verse Paul quotes (Genesis 15:6): God had assured Abraham that, though he and Sarah were long past the age of bearing children, Abraham's offspring would be as many as the stars. Abraham chose to believe and trust in what God said. And so, he was "counted as," or "reckoned as," righteous—justified. That's it. God said something and Abraham chose to trust him. Paul uses banking language here: faith is what led to the credit to Abraham's account. And even the faith Abraham had was not a work but the gift of God.

Later that faith was lived out by Abraham in acts of obedience, but those acts are not what led to the credit into his account. If we are in Christ, by faith in him, we have the same credits to our account.

Romans 4:4–5. Abraham wasn't getting paid for something he earned. He was receiving a gift. This is the God who justifies the ungodly, or we could say "righteous-es the wicked." You cannot earn this kind of righteousness; it only comes by faith.

Romans 4:6–8. Another giant in the history of the Jewish people, David, attests to the gift of God's grace. Instead of crediting our sin against us (notice the accounting language again), God pardons our sins. David had already been justified. His sin, even adultery and murder, did not cancel his justification.

Romans 4:9–12. Abraham was pronounced righteous by God before he ever had the sign of circumcision. In this way, he is also the father of Gentile believers. For the believer, the pronouncement of being justified comes at the beginning, not the end. This order feels backward to us from most things in our culture, where we work and strive and are rewarded with a title, name, or prize only at the end. God names us first, gives us our right standing with him, and then allows us to go forward out of that place. Imagine the freedom it would give you if you believed that you began every day already justified, already good in God's eyes.

Romans 4:13–19. Paul continues and deepens his exploration into the illustration of Abraham as the father of all the faithful. As we can see by the sheer number of verses used to prove his point, Abraham and the issue of law/works/circumcision was a big deal to Paul's audience. But the Bible speaks to us as well, Gentile believers in the twenty-first century. As Paul reminds us at the end of this section, we can be sure that the story of Abraham and his faith is our story as well, and it is intended to strengthen our faith.

In verse 17, Paul quotes Genesis 17:5. Notice the use of the past tense. This is not a mistake; the same thing is found in the Hebrew in Genesis. God speaks about making Abraham the father of many nations as if it has already happened, because in the mind of God, it already has. Abraham's and Sarah's bodies had passed the time of fertility and in terms of reproduction were both technically dead. This is the sense in which the phrase "the God…who gives life to the dead" is used here. New life for Sarah was an impossibility, a dream that had likely died decades before.

Isaac did not yet exist, but God called him into existence. There was no Israel, nor any thought of such a thing in anyone's mind. Yet this great nation was already conceived in the mind of God, complete with Isaac and Jacob, the family line of David, and all of the stories of rescue that we know today as a window into the heart of God. All of this sprang forth from an old man's body and an old woman's womb. Things are not always as they seem to our human eyes. The plan of God is sometimes surprising and even shocking.

Romans 4:20–21. This was not an instance of "letting go and letting God." Abraham did not mindlessly wander through this monumental season of his life. He considered his physical inability and his wife's age and years of infertility. Then he considered the promise of his God. He actively weighed one against the other and found God's word about this situation to be more trustworthy than what he saw with his eyes. Faith like this is not irrational; it is choosing to trust what or who is trustworthy.

Furthermore, Abraham's belief was not merely a generic belief "in God." It was a specific trusting of God to do what he had said he would do—give Abraham a son, and many sons. In this way we are like Abraham when we trust God for specific things he has said, has done, and will do. A sweeping, inclusive, blanket belief "in God" is not what grows our faith and relationship with him. We don't trust in an idea. We trust a person to do specific things he has promised. Though God does not speak promises to us in an audible voice, he has given us many promises in his Word.

Romans 4:22–25. The pattern is the same for us as it was for Abraham. We are credited with righteousness by faith. We who stand on the other side of the cross believe the promise, just as Abraham did. He believed that God would keep his promise to bless him, looking forward. We believe God will bless us as well, as we look both back at the cross and forward to our resurrection. If you are in Christ, you are a son or daughter of Abraham, bound up in his family of faith, with Christ's goodness credited to your account.

Reflection Questions

5. In Romans 3:9–18, Paul quotes five different Old Testament passages to prove his point about how far-reaching sin is for all humanity. What does this demonstrate to us about the importance of the connection of the Old Testament and the New Testament in understanding the full story of the Bible? Have you viewed it this way?

6. Because no one is righteous, God had to make peace between himself and us through Jesus. Faith is us resting in this righteousness that has been given to us. What does it look like to rest in this righteousness? What makes it hard for you to rest in it?

7. Abraham was called righteous not because of his behavior or sinlessness but because of who his faith was resting on. Do you evaluate your faith based on how much of it you have or based on what you are trusting in? Why?

8. God, who "gives life to the dead and calls into existence the things that do not exist," miraculously kept his promises made to Abraham. What comfort and encouragement do you get from the story of Abraham and Sarah? What does it show you about God's character?

9. The thought that you are only righteous because of your faith in Jesus can be a big concept to wrap your head around. Over your time as a believer, what has helped you to absorb this truth and apply it in deeper ways?

Focus verse

As it is written, "None is righteous, no, not one; no one understands; no one seeks for God. All have turned aside; together they have become worthless; no one does good, not even one."

Romans 3:10–12

Reflections, curiosities, frustrations:

Study 3

Christ Died for Us

Read Romans 5

Observation Questions

1. According to Romans 5:1–11, what things does our faith give us access to?

2. Through our union with Christ, what does suffering produce in our lives?

3. According to Romans 5:12–19, what things came through Adam? What things came through Christ?

4. Paul uses the phrase "free gift" five times in Romans 5:15–17. What is Paul describing, and why is this an appropriate description of it?

Interpretation

The word *therefore* is a huge clue in Paul's writing. It tells us that everything we've just read has led up to this new point he's about to make. Paul has explained at length that the gospel is altogether different from any other way of life, that it is not obtained by works or the law but by faith, as illustrated by the lives of Abraham and David. Paul is explaining what this means for us now, we who together as Jews and Gentiles have been justified. It means that we have both peace with God and access to him.

Romans 5:1–2. This is the language of the temple. Access to the Holy of Holies, the innermost part of the temple, was granted only once a year, and then only to a priest. It was such a holy place that a rope was tied around the ankle of the priest so that if he were struck down during his worship, he could be pulled out without anyone else having to go in and risk their life as well. To this place, the most sacred place of intimacy with the living and creating God, we have been given entrance.

Romans 5:3–5. These sufferings are not just everyday aches and pains of living in a fallen world. These are persecution and opposition—literally, "pressures"— that come from living in a world hostile to Jesus. These pressures produce what can be translated as "a bearing up under it." The antagonism of the world pushes us down, and we stand firm under it. This often-painful process produces character as the Lord transforms us to be like himself. Suffering is the path to glory for the believer. It is the hope that God can enable us to thrive even in hard places.

Romans 5:6–8. Powerless, sickly, unable to do anything for ourselves, helpless, ungodly—all of these are in the range of meaning for the word translated "weak" in verse 6. We were not exactly a prize when God came for us. We were sinners, his enemies, hostile, and powerless. The greatness of the gift and the unworthiness of the recipients show the immensity of the love God pours out. We were not the initiators in this transaction. All of the pursuit is on the part of the one who has never needed us but loves us nonetheless.

Romans 5:9–11. We exist now in the already–not yet condition of those belonging to a kingdom that has not yet reached its fullness. How can we, the subjects, be sure of his future mercy? God has already done the most difficult work of reconciling us to himself, making us righteous by the blood of Jesus. Surely he will finish this work of bringing us to the end of time and into his courts, to the full embrace of a beloved daughter by a merciful king.

Romans 5:12. Paul interrupts himself. If he were to have finished his thought, it probably would have read something like, "Just as through one man sin entered the world, and death through sin, and so death came to all because all shared his sin, so also through one man righteousness entered the world, and life through righteousness, and so life came to all because all shared his righteousness." In this passage, Paul is tying together the roles of Adam, the first man, who here represents all humanity in their sin, and Christ, who is called "the last Adam" (1 Corinthians 15:45) and who saves all humanity by his obedience. With precise logic, Paul shows us our own failure in Adam and our freedom in Christ.

Romans 5:13–14. What is the relationship between sin and law? Was there sin in the world before there was a law to name it? Paul answers yes and that sin led to death, even before there were commands with a penalty attached.

Romans 5:15–17. Though both Jesus and Adam represent all of the people of the world by their actions (Jesus by obedience and Adam by sin), the contrast between them is stunning. As John Calvin writes, "Christ is much more powerful to save than Adam was to destroy."[1] When Adam sinned, because he represented all of humanity, all fell. Generations of sinners came from him. The grace of God does not simply cancel out the sin of Adam as with a one-to-one ratio; rather, God's grace is so much more. The sin of Adam deserved condemnation; this is logical and expected. We might think that if one person's (Adam's) sin deserved judgment, then the many sins and guilt of untold numbers of generations would be answered by much *more* judgment—layers and layers of judgment. But instead, that weighty pile of guilt is answered by God's free grace. All those sins—past and future—were completely wiped out by one act, Jesus's death. As John Stott writes, "Grace operates a different arithmetic."[2]

Paul goes on to say that not only did Jesus move us from the place where death reigned (literally, "ruled") to the place of life by giving us his righteousness, but he actually moved us to the position of future rulers, reigning through Jesus. Believers will participate in the resurrection and somehow have a share in the Lord's kingdom. This is an awesome exchange of positions. This is the weight God gives to us, to our humanity, to the image of himself in which we are made. In some way, we will rule. This is our absolutely secure future—co-rulers in a vast kingdom of peace and perfection. This can have a huge impact on our perspective of the influence and seemingly small place we may occupy in the here and now.

Romans 5:18–19. Here is where we see our connection to Adam. Our western minds have a hard time with the Hebrew concept of corporate personality, but the unity of the human race was obvious to biblical writers. The writer of Hebrews speaks of Levi still being in the loins of his ancestor Abraham (Hebrews 7:9–10). And when Achan stole Jericho's treasure, the Lord was angry at all of Israel (Joshua 7:1). Adam *was* the human race; his very name means "humanity" or "man." What Adam did, his descendants did also. If, therefore, we are all condemned in the first Adam's sin, we who are justified by faith are saved by the death and resurrection of Jesus.

Romans 5:20–21. So what about the law? What was its purpose in this equation of condemnation and salvation, if sin and death already existed on the earth before Moses was ever given the Ten Commandments? The law named sin, quantified it, and brought it clearly out into the light of day.

The law shows us the depth of sin in humanity and our need for a savior. Jesus used the law in this way in his Sermon on the Mount, where he expanded on the Ten Commandments to broaden our understanding of their scope and of how impossible it is to keep them in their entirety.

A note on truths and commands: At this point you may be asking yourself why Paul hasn't told us to do anything yet. We are five chapters in, and there hasn't been a command yet. This is very much on purpose. Paul takes five full chapters to tell us about the indicatives, things that are true about God and about us, before he ever gives an imperative, a command. Why? Because as believers, motivation matters, and we often get the order wrong. We don't obey and serve Jesus in order to get his love and approval; we obey and serve him because we already have it. Paul wants us to know who we are before he ever tells us what to do.

Jesus has given us access by faith to grace, to undeserved preferential treatment by God. Though we all died when our representative, Adam, sinned, we who are in Christ will live through the better Adam, Jesus. Jesus's work not only covers your sin but raises you to reign with Christ. What a remarkable gift, that the Messiah would die for us while we had not yet turned from our sin. This is the extraordinary mercy of our God, the free gift of righteousness.

Reflection Questions

5. Paul calls us to rejoice in suffering because God uses suffering to produce endurance, character, and hope in our lives. Can you think of a time of suffering in your life when you experienced the truth of Romans 5:3–5?

6. When Christ found us, we were powerless, sickly, unable to do anything for ourselves, helpless, ungodly, and weak. We had nothing to offer, and he set his love on us. Does this change your view of yourself before you were a Christian? How does this give you a greater understanding of your salvation?

7. The sin of Adam brought decay and death to every human in history. As Paul says, "death spread to all men." What evidence do you see of this on a physical level and an emotional level? In what areas have you seen this in your own life?

8. Christ's death and resurrection have not just made you righteous but also have given you the position as future rulers with Christ. In what ways does this show how Christ's death did more than undo Adam's sin? How does this encourage you?

9. How have you seen the free gift of the gospel affect your life? In what areas do you long to see more of an impact?

Focus verse

For one will scarcely die for a righteous person—though perhaps for a good person one would dare even to die—but God shows his love for us in that while we were still sinners, Christ died for us.

Romans 5:7–8

Reflections, curiosities, frustrations:

Study 4

Dead to Sin and Alive to God

Read Romans 6 and 7

Observation Questions

1. According to Romans 6:1–11, what benefits are given to us through Christ's death and resurrection?

2. According to Romans 6:15–23, what was our relationship to sin before Christ? What is our relationship with sin now that God has given us eternal life through Christ?

3. In Romans 7:1–6, what relationship with the law does Paul say we now have? What analogy does he use in verses 1–3?

4. Summarize Romans 7:7–25 in a few sentences.

Interpretation

Paul explained to us at the end of chapter 5 how we are permanently linked to Adam. Here he explores our union with Christ, and ultimately our identity in him. He leads us through our transfer of ownership from one master to another. Our first master was sin, cruel and oppressive. Our second is Christ, whose yoke is easy, and who, instead of punishing us, gives us the ultimate gift of freedom and makes us into someone new.

Romans 6:1. These questions are a good litmus test for whether or not we are truly talking about the gospel. Does it seem too good to be true? Does it seem counterintuitive or too free? If what we are preaching or teaching never sounds radical or even a little extreme, then "the likelihood is that we are not preaching Paul's gospel."[1]

Romans 6:2–10. We as believers identify with Christ's death in our baptism (which is an outward physical symbol of an inward spiritual reality). It is a funeral, of sorts. We are "buried" under the waters (whether the sprinkling or immersion waters) into Christ's death. We are then raised with him into life. This is union with Christ.

We died with Christ; we also live with him in his resurrection. We are a new creation now (see 2 Corinthians 5:17). Ownership of an enslaved person ends at death; that is, the enslaver can no longer control the one who is dead. In the same way, Paul is telling us that we died. He says that it is impossible to go back to obeying our old enslaver, sin. We do sin; we may even have habitual sins. But a believer is no longer dominated by sin. Once someone has died with Christ, sin is no longer the truest thing about them.

Romans 6:11–14. If the old, unconverted sinner in us has died, why is Paul warning us against sin in these verses? Why are we sinning at all? When we became believers, our master changed. We are now no longer ruled by sin; it is not what reigns in our hearts. But, like a rogue army still roaming the hills of a conquered nation, unwilling to submit, sin pops up and tries to instigate a rebellion in our hearts. Too often, we give into it. But now we actually have the choice not to sin. We, through the Holy Spirit, can obey Christ as our master, which was not possible before our salvation. Jesus reminds us through many different authors and voices and stories and situations in his Word that our former life of slavery to sin is now over. We are his.

Romans 6:15–19. Paul continues to argue with his imaginary opponent, giving his standard answer—No way! All humans, he says, are either slaves of sin or slaves of righteousness. Paul acknowledges that the analogy of slavery, a human institution, is not completely accurate. Christ is not a taskmaster; we are actually liberated by him. But we still live in this fallen world and must fight temptation. Our freedom from sin is not given so that we can do whatever we want. Freedom from sin is what allows us to become more like Jesus.

Romans 6:20–22. Being a servant of God will inevitably lead to holiness because God will be working in us, revealing our sin, and changing us. But this sanctification, this working out of our salvation, this little by little change into a person totally surrendered to God, does not happen by hard work, by determination, or by self-discipline and careful reminders of "Do not mess up! Be good!" Instead, Paul motivates us to obedience by reminding us of who we are.

We see the temptation to gossip, to pull away in cold silence, to stroke the memory of someone's affirmation of us and replay it in our minds over and over, to continue in whatever sin. But our own efforts at hardcore, cold turkey quitting will not ultimately help us in these places. Instead, Paul wants us to hear our Father speaking in that moment, saying, "You are mine. You are loved. You are being made into someone else—a new creation. I am delighting in you this very minute, singing over you. I know what you are feeling with such intimacy that I know what you'll think before you think it, and I am there with you as you feel it. I am preparing a place for you in my kingdom where you will reign with me. Now, look back at that temptation, you beloved daughter of mine for whom I spilled my Son's blood and for whom he constantly intercedes. I will love you still, no matter what you do. But knowing what you know about who you really are, do you still choose to sin?" *This love,* sisters, is what motivates us to obey.

Romans 6:23. The term "wages" is often used to describe the pay of a soldier. Working in the army of the enemy leads to an incredibly disappointing payment—death. But the gift given to those in union with Christ is eternal life. Death pays wages; you get what you earn. But Christ gives a gift; you get what you do not deserve.

Romans 7:1–3. Paul uses analogies to explain our new relationship to the law. In chapter 6 he explained how we were once slaves to the law but that is no longer the case because of our death with Christ. Now he moves to another, equally powerful analogy—marriage. In Paul's time, women had no power and lived under the law of their husband. Only upon his death was she released from his rule, and subsequently free to marry another.

Romans 7:4–7. We died with Christ so that we would be free from our old husband (the law), marry our new husband (Christ), and produce fruit. The "old written code" (again, the law) was external and had no power to produce life. The New Covenant is of the heart and is life-giving.

If we died to the law and it does not produce life, is the law bad in itself? Is it, in fact, sin? No, Paul answers. We wouldn't even be able to see sin clearly if it weren't exposed and revealed by the law. Paul uses covetousness as an example: he didn't even really see the extent of his sin until the tenth commandment (you shall not covet) made it clear.

Romans 7:8–13. This is the same principle as an ex-smoker who is doing fine until she walks by a No Smoking sign and suddenly has a terrible craving for a cigarette. By nature, the human heart wants what is forbidden. It's not actually the law that is the problem; it's our sin that deceives. The law itself is a declaration of God's will and is therefore good. Because of sin, the law became a destroying power, something that in its own nature it is not.

So do we as believers need to obey the law? Yes and no. Yes, in the sense that the freedom we have in Christ is freedom to serve and produce fruit, not to indulge our every whim. We are, as Paul says, still slaves, but slaves to Christ. No, in the sense that we do not obey in order to be saved and to grow in Christ. We have already been justified, sanctified, and glorified.[2]

Romans 7:14–20. Paul again emphasizes that the law is not the problem. The law is good—spiritual, even. The law, through the Spirit, exposes our motivations. And although he is technically no longer a slave to sin and has a new master, Paul experiences the battle of fighting against sin just as we do. Sin is still living in Paul—literally, "making its home" within him. Though he has been made new, the enemy still camps out within him and is the cause of his struggle. Paul knows that this inclination to disobey is not his truest self but the sin living in him.

Romans 7:21–23. Paul finds a law, here better translated "principle," at work within him: When he tries to take a step toward loving Jesus in some way, he immediately feels a resistance, so that he is at war with himself. Both sin and Christ dwell within us—how would we not feel this conflict?

Romans 7:24–25. This is so frustrating! How will this ever end? Even Paul finds himself divided. At his core, he loves God's thoughts, God's desires, God's law. But his sinful nature, the enemy that still lives within him, does not love God's law. Paul is about to launch us into the beautiful Spirit-filled life in chapter 8. But here he lingers on the struggle that he clearly knows very well. And in so doing, he frees us of any fantasies of a constantly victorious Christian life full of only success and perfect obedience.

Here we find such comfort and truth about obedience and growth as believers: It does not come from determination and hard work. It is never complete, even for the mature Christian. We may think that if we are real, true, or "good" Christians, we shouldn't have so much trouble believing, obeying, or wanting to believe or obey. But Paul tells us here that the struggle is the norm—the evidence, even, of God working in us. For without God's work within us, there would be no struggle against sin at all.

"Thanks be to God through Jesus Christ our Lord!" There is one who will deliver us from our sin. And though the struggle is real while we live here on earth, victory is promised, and is already ours. We have been delivered, are being delivered, and will be delivered from our sin and our fight against it. Therefore we should be encouraged and keep up the fight as we seek to live under our new master—Christ and his righteousness.

Reflection Questions

5. When you think about your spiritual state, do you usually look at yourself as someone who has been set free from sin or someone who is still enslaved to sin? How does what you have learned in this study change your thoughts on that?

6. How would you now explain our relationship to the law as believers?

7. What sin pattern do you struggle the most with in your life (slave of sin)? In what ways or situations have you seen this sin pattern start to lose its grip (slave of righteousness)? What has brought this change about?

8. Paul describes the Christian life as a battle with sin. Even when you don't want to sin, you often do. Do you view your struggle with sin as evidence that God is working in your life and changing you? Why or why not?

9. At the point when Paul is wrestling so much that he cries out, "Wretched man that I am!" looking for a solution to this exhausting, recurring pattern, he gives thanks to God for Jesus. When this is your reaction to sin what is usually the result in your heart and in the situation?

Focus verse

For the death he died he died to sin, once for all, but the life he lives he lives to God. So you must consider yourselves dead to sin and alive to God in Christ Jesus.

Romans 6:10–11

Reflections, curiosities, frustrations:

Study 5

More Than Conquerors

Read Romans 8

Observation Questions

1. According to Romans 8:5–14, what are the differences between living according to the flesh versus living according to the Spirit?

2. What things that the Spirit is doing are listed in Romans 8:15–16 and 26–27?

3. What does Romans 8:28–34 say God will do for his children?

4. What things listed in Romans 8:35–39 will not be able to separate us from the love of God?

Interpretation

At the end of chapter 7, Paul wrote about our struggle against sin. Even as Christians we can be divided, warring within ourselves. And although this is often our experience, God has not left us to fight alone. He has given us his own "secret weapon," an indispensable ally and a guarantee of final victory—the Holy Spirit himself.

Romans 8:1–3. This is a categorical declaration of justification, of being made right with God. There is no going back, says the apostle Paul. You are completely finished with accusation and disapproval directed at you from God; they don't exist. The phrase "likeness of sinful flesh" in verse 3 means neither that Jesus was sinful nor that he was less than fully human. Paul is telling us that God judged our sins in his sinless Son, in whom we are hidden. The power of sin was broken by the perfect humanity of Jesus.

Romans 8:4. This is the goal, the end game, what God hopes for us—that we might fulfill the law (the moral law, that is). Remember how Jesus talks about the law in Matthew 5:17–18: "Do not think that I have come to abolish the Law or the Prophets; I have not come to abolish them but to fulfill them. For truly, I say to you, until heaven and earth pass away, not an iota, not a dot, will pass from the Law until all is accomplished."

The law is good; it is the righteousness, love, and purity of God. Time and time again, Jesus spoke of and expanded upon the Ten Commandments, the greatest laws of loving God and loving others as ourselves. Jesus did not come to get rid of the law. He came to obey it perfectly, because we couldn't.

Romans 8:5–8. Paul explains a division here between those who follow the lead of their own sinful or fallen nature and those who follow the lead of the Spirit.

Depending on which we surrender to, our inner lives look very different. The sinful nature leads to self-centered, self-serving thoughts, is hostile to God, resists his law, cannot please God, and ultimately leads to death. The Spirit, on the other hand, directs the mind to the things of the Spirit and brings life and peace.

Romans 8:9–11. Those who belong to God are "in the Spirit." We do the things that please the Spirit, because the Spirit lives in us. The very Spirit who hovered over the surface of the waters at creation, the Spirit who led Jesus through the wilderness, sustaining him and walking him faithfully through temptation, the Spirit of God who raised Jesus from the dead now lives in you. Not only that, but the same Spirit will give life to our bodies at the resurrection.

Romans 8:12–17. It is by the Spirit that we, to use an old word, "mortify," or put to death, the flesh. We put our sins to death, not by determination alone, but by the Spirit. Here Paul uses the language of family, which will dominate the rest of this chapter. He begins in verse 12 with "brothers," speaking now about family rules, the norms and rhythms of our new family. Notice that the Spirit is not like sin, which deceives and tricks, trapping us into our behavior. The Spirit is more like a shepherd, acting by persuasion. He leads, never forcing but allowing us to follow after him. He does not coerce by fear but leads by love. This is the way of our new family.

Romans 8:18–19. Paul is saying that comparing present suffering to future glory is like comparing apples to oranges. Later he references the pain of childbirth to the actual joy of the baby being born. Can we compare those two? Think about the hours spent laboring or the months spent filling out forms for adoption. Remember the pain they entailed, the stretching and the waiting and the endlessness of it. Rate those hours and days with a level of exertion or unpleasantness. Now consider the feeling of actually holding that child. Does that joy fit on a scale of

1 to 10? Do the pain and the joy compare? Does it seem silly to try to compare them? This is what Paul is telling us. They don't come close to each other.

All of creation waits with "eager longing." The Greek word paints a picture of someone standing on their tiptoes, standing with their head raised, stretching their neck to see what is coming over the horizon.[1]

Romans 8:20–23. This redemption and healing of the universe is somehow tied to our own. God is the actor in this sentence. *He* frustrated all of nature in the Fall and bound its future up with ours. As long as we are living under the Fall, creation is bound to decay, pain, disintegration, and frustration.

We do not know exactly what is to be revealed when our adoption is made complete. We can be sure that it is so glorious, so hopeful, so full of weight and beauty that every limb and gust of wind, every cell and organism, every rare creature and backyard squirrel is pictured here to be paused, poised, ready at any moment to celebrate.

Romans 8:24–27. This is where we live—in the in-between, in the already–not yet, battling our sin yet living with the guarantee of the Holy Spirit, saved from God's wrath but still doing what we don't want to do, looking forward in hope to glory but longing and groaning in the pain of this world. This is the place of sanctification (becoming more like Jesus), where we as believers confidently expect a promised future that will make the despair of this world fade like the pain of childbirth.

As all of creation groans, waiting for our redemption, the Spirit groans with us and over us. He identifies with the church as we wait and long for the final day; he even prays for us, with and without words. We often do not know whether to pray for deliverance from our sufferings or for strength to endure them.[2] And so prayer is a joint effort between the children of God and the Spirit of God.

Romans 8:28–30. These verses are often quoted. Sometimes their familiarity can breed unbelief or cause us to miss what is really being proclaimed. Let's paraphrase them in order to hear them in a fresh way:

The truth is, for those who love God, he is constantly, specifically, and powerfully working on their behalf. He is using their joys, their suffering, their bodies and minds, their network of relationships, their groanings, their diseases, their prayers, and everything in between to increase or advance their well-being, and ultimately their salvation. He has a premeditated, perfectly planned purpose for each of them; in their lives, there are no accidents or missteps on the part of God. For he knew them, which in the mind of God meant that he already loved them. He decided beforehand that they would be his and that he would, through suffering, make them to be like Jesus, both in their character and in their conduct. In God's mind, the change, the transformation, is so sure, so guaranteed, that he speaks of their glorification in the past tense.

Romans 8:31–32. Notice that Paul does not simply ask, Who is against us? He knows very well who and what we battle: indwelling sin; the world that is offended by the cross; our weary, breaking bodies and minds; the powers of darkness; and, until the new earth, death. But the question is this: If the one who ultimately holds judgement in his hands has already decided your fate, if he is already on your side, then whose estimation of you, whose condemnation, whose words or judgement have any power over you?

In verse 32, Paul argues from the greater to the lesser: If God gave up his Son, not sparing him the suffering of hell and total separation from himself, to secure your salvation (the greater), will he not continue to be gracious and generous, giving you exactly what you need (the lesser)? Do not look to your circumstances to be assured of his love for you. Look at the correct place for your encouragement, for your confidence—the cross.

Romans 8:33–34. Again notice that Paul does not ask, Who will accuse us? Most of us spend much of our day warding off accusations—of Satan, of our own doubts, of the past, of others' critical voices. But in this question Paul tells us who we are—God's elect. We are the chosen ones, belonging to God, daughters of the Most High, loved, sung over, pursued, worthwhile, and justified by the only one who can finally justify anyone. Who will accuse in a way that has any weight or meaning in the end? No one.

Because of the death of Christ, no one can condemn the Christian. He not only died but was raised and even now prays for us. Jesus prays for you specifically, probably by name. Who will condemn the one whose name is written in the Book of Life? No one.

Romans 8:35–37. And here is the fundamental question, what we fear behind all other fears: Will my soul survive these overwhelming trials? Will the guarantee, the hope, the security I know in Christ, ever be taken away? Can I be separated from that faithful loving-kindness? Paul quotes Psalm 44:22, a psalm of Israel's persecution, where they have been faithful to God and his covenant but he nevertheless allowed them to struggle, to be mocked, stressed, and spread apart as a people, and to feel as if they'd been abandoned. But, Paul says, even in his seeming absence, God has not taken his love from us.

Romans 8:38–39. Paul ends his crescendo of amazing confidence that we will never be left alone in our suffering by listing the extremes of human experience. Death itself, invisible spiritual powers, things we don't even know about yet—nothing can loosen the grip Jesus has on us.

If we are in Christ, there is no accusation, disapproval, or blame for us from God. We have been given life and peace, have been made sons and daughters and heirs with Christ. We will suffer with Jesus and will be raised from the dead. Then, we will be glorified with him, a triumph on a scale of which we do not yet have the capacity to dream. We groan and the creation groans with us as we wait. The Spirit helps us pray. God works all for our good, transforming us into the image of Jesus. He justifies, vindicates, intercedes, and holds us in and through all things. This is the overwhelming mercy, security, and faithfulness of our God.

Reflection Questions

5. "The very Spirit who hovered over the surface of the waters at creation, the Spirit who led Jesus through the wilderness, sustaining him and walking him faithfully through temptation, the Spirit of God who raised Jesus from the dead now lives in you." How does this truth help you when you wrestle with your sin?

6. Paul explains that the suffering that we experience in this life does not compare to the glory we will experience in the next. How does that thought help you in your current suffering? What part of that thought is hard to connect to?

7. Paul talks about the Spirit groaning over us and praying for us as well as Jesus praying for us. Did you know that the Spirit and Jesus were doing these things for you? What about that is comforting to you?

8. How can looking at and thinking on what God did for us through the cross impact our view of what God will do for us in the "little things" in our daily lives?

9. Many things can happen in this life, but none of them have the ability to separate us from God's love for us. How does this change your view of the ultimate impact of the trials and suffering you have experienced or will experience?

Focus verse

For I am sure that neither death nor life, nor angels nor rulers, nor things present nor things to come, nor powers, nor height nor depth, nor anything else in all creation will be able to separate us from the love of God in Christ Jesus our Lord.

Romans 8:38–39

Reflections, curiosities, frustrations:

Study 6

Not Human Will, but God's Choice

Read Romans 9

Observation Questions

1. In Romans 9:4–5, what does Paul say belongs to Israel?

2. According to Romans 9:6–18, what or who determines whether God shows mercy or compassion?

3. Summarize what Paul is saying in Romans 9:19–23 about God and what he has created.

4. What issue is Paul addressing in Romans 9:30–32?

Interpretation

At the end of chapter 8, we were enjoying the amazing truth that God's hold on us can never be loosened. He chooses us, molds us, and sets his love on us all the way to our perfection in the new heavens and the new earth. Now Paul anticipates the question that must have lurked in the minds of his contemporaries: If God is so trustworthy, if he supposedly doesn't let go once you are his, then what happened to the Jews? Weren't they supposed to be his special people? Didn't he abandon them? Paul walks us through the problem of his own people and their God.

Romans 9:1–5. Obviously Paul could not forfeit his salvation for his people, but his anguish for them tells us that he would have been willing. In Exodus 32, Moses prays something similar for the same nation. These are the covenant people of God, chosen from all the nations of the world to be his special people. Paul lists eight privileges that came with the designation of "chosen nation": (1) the adoption as sons, (2) the divine glory, (3) the covenants, (4) the law, (5) temple worship, (6) the promises, (7) the patriarchs, and (8) the ancestry of Christ. All of these were intended to prepare Israel, to educate them about the plan and intentions of God to rescue them with the Messiah. One would think that such a privileged people, prepared for centuries with these pointers to Christ, would recognize and celebrate the Messiah when he finally arrived.[1]

They didn't. For the most part, they totally missed him. Was this God's fault?

Romans 9:6–13. In fact, it was not God's fault, says Paul, because not all Israel is really Israel, at least in the spiritual sense. God told Abraham in Genesis 22 that although Ishmael was also his son, God would use Isaac to build the nation. Isaac had been promised to Abraham earlier (Genesis 18) and given through Sarah, although she was barren and long past child-bearing age. Therefore, Isaac is called the child of promise, as opposed to the child of flesh, borne by Hagar.

God chooses as he will, regardless of actions or some sort of merit. Jacob and Esau were children of the same mother, the same father, grown in the same womb at the same time. Neither could have shown themselves to be superior or more deserving than the other. Before they were even born, God declared one favored, telling Rebekah that the older would serve the younger even though that would be against their culture's norms. This didn't necessarily mean that Esau, the individual, would serve Jacob but that Esau's eventual people, his descendants, would serve Jacob's. And they did—for long periods of time the Edomites (Esau's descendants) were in some sort of servitude to either Israel or Judah. "Esau I hated" does not mean a literal hatred for Esau but is a Hebrew idiom meaning that Esau would not experience God's favor.

Romans 9:14–16. So that doesn't seem fair. Esau didn't even have a chance. Before he ever took a breath, his fate was already decided—he wasn't the chosen son. Is God a cruel tyrant? A puppet master who enjoys the show? The quote here is from Exodus 33, when Moses was leading the Israelites in the wilderness. He was striving to lead them well and asked God to show him (Moses) his glory. God responded by saying that he would make all of his goodness pass before Moses and would proclaim his name, "the Lord." And then he says these words: "And I will be gracious to whom I will be gracious, and will show mercy on whom I will show mercy." Paul explains to us that all favor lies in the choice of God, not in any sort of work or effort on our part.

A note on fairness: To the ears of Americans, who understand humans to have certain unalienable rights, all of this might seem quite unfair, cruel even. But before we define "fair" in this circumstance, let's first establish a baseline. The given for human beings—flawed, broken, affected by our first parents, sinners, incredibly offensive to God and his holiness—is hell. That is fair. What we all deserve, without the intervention of a Savior, is eternal wrath and punishment. We read in John 3:16–18 (emphasis added),

> For God so loved the world, that he gave his only Son, that whoever believes in him should not perish but have eternal life. For God did not send his Son into the world to condemn the world, but in order that the world might be saved through him. Whoever believes in him is not condemned, but *whoever does not believe is condemned already,* because he has not believed in the name of the only Son of God.

From conception, we are sinners—"condemned already," says John. God has no obligation to rescue any of us. The fact that he intervenes and chooses to save some is an act of sheer mercy.

Romans 9:17–18. In Exodus 9, Pharaoh and the Egyptians were in the middle of the plagues. God told Moses to say to Pharaoh,

> For by now I could have put out my hand and struck you and your people with pestilence, and you would have been cut off from the earth. But for this purpose I have raised you up, to show you my power, so that my name may be proclaimed in all the earth.

God chooses whomever he wants and shows who he is and his own mercy in the process. This is neither cruel nor unfair, as we will see in the next verses. But in order to hear these words as what they are—God's words and a revelation of who God is—we have to keep in mind the backdrop from earlier in Paul's letter to the Romans. In chapter 3 he quotes Psalm 14: "None is righteous, no, not one; no one understands; no one seeks for God." And he writes in Romans 3:23, "for all have sinned and fall short of the glory of God." This is our natural state of being before God's intervention—lost, sinful, and running in the opposite direction of God. It is not his judgement that should shock us but his mercy.

Romans 9:19–24. Paul just explained that God is the one who makes decisions about who receives wrath and who receives mercy. Our minds may logically come to this question: How is it that we are held responsible when God is the one who chooses? Paul answers first by explaining that God has the right of a craftsman over his work to decide its use. Consider a lump of clay on the wheel asking the potter as she spins it into a shape, "Why are you making me into a bowl? I wanted to be a vase!" Neither do we, God's creatures, have sufficient wisdom to judge our creator.[2]

How are we to understand the phrase "prepared for destruction" in verse 22? Is this blind fatalism where God arbitrarily chooses everyone's destiny and nothing we do makes any difference? No. Paul's point is that sinful human beings prepare *themselves* for destruction, and God endures their rebellion with great patience until the day of his wrath.

Romans 9:25–26. As a picture of God's love for Israel, God told Hosea to marry an unfaithful wife, Gomer. Her children, born of other men, were named as measures of where Israel was in its relationship to God. A daughter was born and named No Mercy, because God said he would not have mercy on Israel. A son was named Not My People, because God had rejected the people of Israel. The people, like Gomer, had been totally unfaithful, and God had given them up to their own choices and destruction.

And then something amazing happened. Out of his own compassion and mercy, for no reason other than he wanted to do it, God turned the entire picture around.

In Hosea 2, God allured Israel, speaking tenderly, calling Israel back to himself. And then the children who were named No Mercy and Not My People were renamed Beloved and My People. Paul quotes Hosea here to explain that this is how God shows the riches of his glory, even to Gentiles, who were not originally a part of God's people.

Romans 9:27–30. Again Paul speaks of God's mercy, this time from the Book of Isaiah. After an Assyrian invasion was used by God to judge the nation who had turned away from him, Isaiah spoke of God's mercy in allowing even a small remnant of Israel to survive. God had promised that the nation coming from Abraham would be like the sand on the seashore in number. Because of their sin and rebellion, only a small portion of Israel would be saved. However, divine mercy prevented their total obliteration.

The word "pursue" in verse 30 is used in the sense of an athletic contest, where the prize is righteousness. The Jews ran the race by working hard to justify themselves, while the Gentiles looked only to Christ for their justification. And this brings us to the stumbling stone. It looked to the Jews as if the Gentiles had not even run the race but had won the prize nevertheless.[3]

In the last portion of verse 33, Paul puts together two prophecies from Isaiah (Isaiah 8:14 and 49:23) to show that most of the nation of Israel rejected the very person who was to become the cornerstone of their faith. But why do so many stumble over Jesus? Why do we find protection in him as our refuge? Why didn't the Jews recognize him as the ultimate sacrifice and sanctuary? Because the cross, and Jesus himself, is offensive. The cross "undermines our self-righteousness."[4]

We do not want to humble ourselves and admit how much help we need. The truth is, we do not need a little help, a new outlook, a paradigm shift, a better attitude, or more energy; we need a savior, which implies an incredible lack and brokenness at the core of who we are.

Reflection Questions

5. According to Romans 9:11b, God chooses as he wills, regardless of actions or some sort of merit. What about that is comforting to you? What about it is frustrating?

6. The Jews pursued righteousness that depended more on what they could do right religiously than on faith. Can you think of an instance this week when you have looked righteous but it wasn't a righteousness that depended on faith?

7. Paul makes it clear that God is the creator or the potter and we are the clay. Who are we to tell him what to do with his creation? When have you wrestled with this and judged God for the choices he has made with his creation?

8. Paul uses Scriptures from Isaiah and Hosea to show God's compassion and mercy. How was thinking on those Scriptures helpful in the midst of trying to understand God's sovereign choice when it comes to salvation?

9. The cross is offensive and a stumbling block. What about the cross offends you most?

Focus verse

What shall we say then? Is there injustice on God's part? By no means! For he says to Moses, "I will have mercy on whom I have mercy, and I will have compassion on whom I have compassion." So then it depends not on human will or exertion, but on God, who has mercy.

Romans 9:14–16

Reflections, curiosities, frustrations:

Study 7

Preach the Good News

Read Romans 10

Observation Questions

1. According to Romans 10:1–4, what were the Jews doing that was keeping them from God?

2. In Romans 10:9–13, what does Paul say you have to do to be saved?

3. According to Romans 10:14–15, what are some ways the gospel is made known to the lost?

4. In Romans 10:18–21, Paul is quoting four different Old Testament passages (verse 18: Psalm 19:4; verse 19: Deuteronomy 32:21; verse 20: Isaiah 65:1; verse 21: Isaiah 65:2). Summarize what these verses are saying.

Interpretation

Paul just walked us through some staggering declarations about God's sovereignty: God chooses, God hardens, God is in control. But what about our humanity? Don't we even have a choice? What about human responsibility? As he reasons through Israel's failed relationship with God, Paul explains to us that we do, indeed, have responsibility in this relationship—to confess our sin, to believe the gospel, and to trust our Father.

Romans 10:1–4. Paul must have understood the Romans' zeal, as he was extremely zealous himself as a Jew, even to the point of persecuting the church. The Jews were seeking to establish their own righteousness through the law. What does it mean that Christ is the "end of the law"? This "end" can be understood both in the sense of "goal" and in the sense of "conclusion." Christ tells us in Matthew 5:17 that he has come to fulfill the law; his righteousness was perfect, which was the goal. At the same time, since Christ achieved the end, allowing us all to be counted righteous in him, the role of the law as a way to gain righteousness has come to its conclusion.

Romans 10:5–8. Paul's knowledge of the Old Testament Scriptures is astounding. Here he is quoting Moses from two different passages to make his point that salvation comes from faith and that even Moses taught this. Paul paraphrases and then quotes Deuteronomy 30 to explain that the righteousness of God is actually attainable, that it is, in fact, very near. He is telling us, You don't have to scale mountains and swim the deep sea in order to find Christ and his righteousness. Moses was telling the Israelites the same thing in the original passage: the Word of God and the command he is giving you is not so far off that you have to go searching for it. This is what is so remarkable about Christianity as opposed to all other religions of the world. It is not hard work, pilgrimages, meditation, or following a law that leads to righteousness; instead, it is trust in another's work on our behalf. This is also the way of growth in the Christian life—confession, believing the gospel, and trusting your Father.

Romans 10:9–11. "Jesus is Lord" was the first creed of Christians. Paul uses the Greek word *kurios*, which in the Old Testament was the personal name of God, Yahweh, claiming supreme authority over the world.[1] This was a provocative claim during the time that this letter was written, as the caesars of Rome also used the title *kurios.* The word *confess,* when used about sin, means to agree with God, to say the same thing about your sin that he does. When used in a creedal sense, as it is here, it means to say the same thing about God as other believers do.[2]

Paul quotes Isaiah 28:16 again, as he already did in Romans 9:33. In the original context of the Book of Isaiah, God was promising a cornerstone, a tested and sure foundation that God's remnant could trust. While the English Standard Version (ESV) translates this verse "will never be put to shame," the New International Version (NIV) says, "the one who relies on it will never be stricken with panic." While we as believers who trust in Jesus do, of course, experience anxiety and sometimes even panic about things of this world, there is no worry for us about our ultimate safety and salvation. Having believed and put our trust in Christ, we are secure in him.

Romans 10:12–13. The word "for" at the beginning of this verse tells us that Paul is referring to his statement in verse 11. When it comes to salvation, there is no hierarchy for Jews and Gentiles. Whatever differences there were culturally and even in terms of being God's chosen people, all were sinners in need of rescue.

The "riches" that the Lord will give to everyone who calls on him are the same ones that Paul mentions in Romans 2:4, where he is talking about God's judgment on the moral pagans of the day. He condemns them for their hypocrisy in judging others for the very things they themselves do. Then he asks, "Or do you presume on the riches of his kindness and forbearance and patience, not knowing that God's kindness is meant to lead you to repentance?" The riches available to all who call on the name of the Lord are his patience and kindness that lead to repentance. Instead of wrath and judgment, those who cry out to him receive forbearance.

Romans 10:14–16. First-century Rome was a world very different from ours. There were no Bibles lying around thrift stores or in the drawers of hotel rooms. The only Scripture was on scrolls that were housed in synagogues. Since there was not yet a New Testament to be read, the only way Jews or Gentiles could learn about Jesus and the Christian faith was by listening to a believer talk about Jesus's actions and about what he taught while on earth. Even today, though God sometimes chooses to call some of his children initially through their reading of the Bible alone, the primary way he brings his sheep into the fold is through the preaching of the Word, be it formal or not, by his people. This means that the sovereign God of the universe, who formed every cell in our bodies and who reigns in blinding holiness, has chosen to use us—weak, sinful, broken, stuttering people—to explain his lovingkindness to the people in our daily path. It also means that he calls us to bring them in contact with his message, to bring them to places where his Word is preached by his ordained ambassadors. Of course he could save them in an instant, through dreams or visions, or perhaps an angelic visitation. Sometimes he chooses to do so. But we, the church, are the primary way our God chooses to save people.

Without television, newspapers, or the internet, a herald who would stand in the marketplace or city square was the major means of transmitting information in the ancient world. The word "preaching" in verse 14 refers to this act of standing in a public place and announcing the news. And what is the news they are proclaiming? Here Paul quotes Isaiah 52:7, when heralds were sent to the city of

Jerusalem to declare the wonderful news that the Babylonian captivity was finally over. The physical restoration of the city was at hand; this was good news! Sadly, the good news of spiritual restoration to the Jews was not met with the same joy. Paul again quotes Isaiah, but this time he speaks of the way Israel would reject the suffering servant in Isaiah 53.

Romans 10:17–18. This hearing is not passive, like hearing music in the background as you do chores around the house. This is a hearing with understanding, a hearing that changes something in us, that awakens faith. This can only happen by the work of the Holy Spirit.

Paul comes here to a new line of questioning: Is this where things went wrong with Israel? Did they not get the chance to hear about Christ? Is that why they have not believed the gospel? He answers his own question with a quote from Psalm 19, comparing the proclamation of the gospel to the universal witness of the stars. By the time Paul was writing to the Roman church, the gospel had been taught in most of the synagogues and areas where Jews of the ancient world lived. Paul always went to his Jewish brothers first. For years, the gospel had been explained over and over to Paul's own people using Old Testament passages. And it had been rejected again and again. Paul would love to find some excuse for the Jews as to why they had not believed. But the message had so thoroughly covered the Jewish population by this time that Paul compares it to the availability of the view of a starry night sky to anyone who would look up.

Romans 10:19–20. Maybe the Jews didn't understand the gospel? Nope, that excuse won't work either, says Paul. Isaiah foretold that the Gentiles, who were not God's people, would become God's people. To the Jews, the Gentiles would have been considered foolish. They didn't have the prophets, the law, the traditions of centuries of following after Yahweh. And yet God used these "foolish" people to make the Jews jealous, as they proved to be more responsive to the gospel than his chosen people. In fact, we read here that after hundreds of years of being in the dark when it came to a knowledge of God, the Gentiles actually heard and understood the message. Although they were not even seeking after him, God allowed himself to be found by them.

Romans 10:21. Oh, the humility and the grief of our God toward those he loves. Here we see a picture of God, like a patient parent, holding out his arms, pleading, waiting, longing to hold his people, to comfort them, to be their God. Over and over he is rejected. Paul is out of excuses for his Jewish brethren. It is their stubborn hearts that have kept them from believing. And over this unbelief, we feel God's dismay.

Reflection Questions

5. Paul quotes the Old Testament to demonstrate the depth of his knowledge as well as show how the Bible is all connected. How have you viewed the relationship between the Old and New Testaments? How has Paul's use of the Old Testament helped you see the Bible as one cohesive story?

6. It is not the law or all the other things Israel was relying on that secures us in the ultimate saving faith; rather, it is defining sin as God defines it and confessing Jesus as Lord. What do you find amazing about this?

7. Of all the ways God could spread the truth of the gospel, he chooses to preach the Word through human voices. Did you realize how powerful sharing the gospel is? What gets in the way of you doing it?

8. The Jews struggled to believe that salvation was coming through faith and not through perfect adherence to the law, and this led many of them to stumble and reject the gospel. How do you stumble over the question of faith versus works for salvation? Can you relate with their struggle?

9. Write a prayer to the Lord for a lost family member or friend, no matter how far off they seem from the gospel. Pray that God will call them and that he would use you to draw them into his salvation.

Focus verse

But how are they to call on him in who they have not believed? And how are they to believe in him of whom they have never heard? And how are they to hear without someone preaching?

Romans 10:14

Reflections, curiosities, frustrations:

Study 8

Has God Rejected His People?

Read Romans 11

Observation Questions

1. What argument does Paul use in Romans 11:1–6 to show that God has not rejected Israel?

2. According to Romans 11:11–15, what resulted for the Gentiles because of the Jews' rejection of the gospel? What is the warning given to the Gentiles in Romans 11:17–21?

3. According to Romans 11:23–32, what will happen to Israel?

4. How is God described in Romans 11:33–36?

Interpretation

In chapter 9, we read of God's absolute sovereignty and authority in choosing whom he will, when he will. In chapter 10, Paul went on to explain humanity's responsibility to respond to God as he reveals himself. At the end of chapter 10, all seemed bleak. Israel had rejected the Messiah, and God was left holding out his arms to stubborn people who refused his love through Christ. But the story isn't over; God has not and will not give up on Israel. In this section, Paul conveys God's magnificent generosity, as he uses Israel's temporary hardness of heart to widen the open door to the kingdom of light.

Romans 11:1–6. Paul uses himself as the first example of God's faithfulness to the Jews and the fact that God has not given up on his people. Paul was once so bent on punishing the followers of Jesus that he personally oversaw their capture and punishment. But when Jesus revealed himself to Paul on the road to Damascus, he turned this persecutor of the church into an apostle.

Paul gives us another reason to believe God hasn't given up on his people in the story of Elijah. Elijah lived during the time when Ahab was king in Israel. Ahab, who reigned in the northern kingdom for twenty-two years, did "more evil in the sight of the Lord than all who were before him" (1 Kings 16:33). If ever there was a time to despair for those who believed in God, this was it. Of course Elijah felt alone, scared, and like he was the only one left.

God's answer to Elijah was that there were others like him, sustained by the Lord. In fact, there were 7,000 that had not worshiped Baal and who remained faithful to God. Just when it seemed that the end of all belief, the end of all of true Israel was imminent, God let Elijah see that his people were far from extinction. And so here Paul tells us that in the same way God has preserved a remnant, chosen by grace. God was not done with Israel. Even this small number of Jews who believed the gospel were chosen by grace, a clear sign of God's faithfulness.

Romans 11:7–12. Using a combination of three Old Testament passages (Deuteronomy 29, Isaiah 29, and Psalm 69), Paul explains that God gave his people up to their own stubbornness. So what does this mean? Does Israel's stumbling get them kicked out of the kingdom permanently? Paul answers with his consistent "No way!" Israel's fall, as we saw in the illustration of Elijah, was not total, and in verses 11–12, we see that it was not final either. In fact, Paul says, through the Jews' rejection of Jesus, the Gentiles have been saved in order to make Israel jealous of what they see.

So, if the Jews' sin leads to outsiders being let into such a rich kingdom, what wonderful things will happen when the Jews actually obey and believe? Paul uses the phrase "full inclusion" when he speaks of the future of Israel. We do not know how it will start or in what century, but at some point in the future, the nation of Israel will experience a large-scale conversion to Christ. Can you imagine the joy on that day? What amazing pleasure for the Gentile Christians (anyone who is not a Jew) to watch as the hope of the kingdom spreads through the Jewish people and they embrace the true Messiah.

Romans 11:13–15. Paul now addresses the Gentiles directly, explaining the mysterious mercy of God's plan. It's as if he's saying to the church in Rome, I know you think I am only the apostle to the Gentiles, but I have an even greater goal: to make my brothers so jealous as they see what you have that they eventually convert! And again Paul alludes to something more, something spectacular, which he calls "life from the dead" (verse 15).

Israel was supposed to be a beacon of hope for the world, the means by which all nations would know of the goodness of God. They had failed, and God could have simply set them aside. But this is not the way of our God. Instead, God used the failure of his own people as an opportunity to save more. God has not and will never abandon his chosen nation, Israel.

Romans 11:16–20. Here, Paul creates a metaphor of all of God's people throughout the ages as an olive tree. The root of the tree is the patriarchs—people like Abraham, Isaac, and Jacob, those to whom God revealed himself in ages past. The trunk, or stem, is all of those who have believed in the God of Israel over the centuries—think of David, the faithful kings like Josiah and Asa, Ezra, Isaiah, and Anna and Simeon in the temple. Paul, as a Jewish believer, is one of the first fruits of this tree.

Paul goes on to explain that though the Gentiles were never a part of the original tree, God, in his mercy, has grafted some wild Gentile branches onto the tree. When an olive tree in the ancient Near East stopped bearing fruit, one of the ways that the farmer might seek to reinvigorate the fruitless tree was to graft in a wild olive shoot. This would stimulate the further production of fruit for the entire natural plant. Paul is explaining that Israel had stopped producing fruit, and that God had therefore broken off some of his people (the branches) and grafted in a wild shoot (Gentiles).

But don't get arrogant about being a part of the tree, Paul says to the Gentiles in the church at Rome. There are hundreds and hundreds of years of stability and faithfulness of God to the tree (Israel). Your life and faith is rooted in their history.

Romans 11:21–24. During this era in Rome, Jews were despised, persecuted, and sometimes treated with violence. It would have been a real temptation for Gentile Christians to follow their culture and treat their Jewish brothers and sisters with disdain. Paul deflates their arrogance in verse 21 by reminding them that they, too, can be broken off if they fall into unbelief. Long-suffering and endurance are the test of the Christian faith. This is a warning to the Roman church and to us. Complacency has no place in the life of a Christian. This is also an encouragement to the Jews: If God can graft in the wild shoot of the Gentiles, surely he can also graft back in the branches that have been broken off.

Romans 11:25–29. Israel had been hardened for a period of time in order that the rest of the nations may be brought in, and ultimately so that all of Israel may be saved. Paul uses passages from Isaiah to declare the future salvation of his brethren.

How are the Jewish people enemies and beloved at the same time? This speaks to the fact that the present hardening of the Jews is temporary. Right now, says Paul, the Jews are enemies of God so that you (Gentiles) might be saved, but ultimately, they will be brought back in.

The word "irrevocable" in verse 29 is the key to all of chapters 9–11. God's promises to Israel are irreversible, unalterable, final, and binding. He could no more renege on his promises to them than he could cease being God. The fulfillment of these promises looks different than anyone may have imagined. But they hold true; the nation of Israel is still special to God.

Mercy is the posture of God toward the Jew and Gentile sinners who have, in different eras, rejected him. In verse 32 we read that word "all" again. Here, "all Israel will be saved" means that both Jews and Gentiles will be saved, not that every single Israelite will be saved. Sin, disobedience, and failure are not final, not even for the Jews.

Romans 11:33–36. Eleven chapters of explaining human nature and God's nature, God's redemption, the struggle against sin, the work of the Spirit, and Israel's future now tied up with the destiny of the Gentiles leads Paul to an outburst of worship. What is there to do after such revelation but to worship the God who cannot be counseled, who owes nothing to anyone, who is the source, the means, and the goal of everything on earth? The more we understand about this unsearchably wise God, the more we are led to worship him.

Reflection Questions

5. In Romans 11:1, Paul references how God radically changed him as a sign of God's faithfulness. Read Acts 8:1–3 and 9:1–19. In light of who we know Paul to be in Romans, what elements of his conversion are surprising to you?

6. Israel's unbelief opened the door for God to show mercy by extending salvation to the Gentiles. What are your thoughts on God using something so heartbreaking for the good of the Gentiles?

7. Paul takes several verses to describe the pruning of the unbelieving Jews and the grafting in of the believing Gentiles, both of which enable the tree to grow and thrive. What part of this analogy stood out to you the most?

8. While Israel has rejected God, God will not renege on his promise to bring salvation to some of the Jews. What does this show us about the character and humility of God? How are you different than him?

9. In Romans 11:33–36, Paul paints a beautiful picture of God, describing many of his main attributes. Which of these attributes is the most comforting and connecting for you as you think about God?

Focus verse

Oh, the depth of the riches and wisdom and knowledge of God! How unsearchable are his judgments and how inscrutable his ways! For who has known the mind of the Lord, or who has been his counselor? Or who has given a gift to him that he might be repaid? For from him and through him and to him are all things. To him be glory forever. Amen.

Romans 11:33–36

Reflections, curiosities, frustrations:

Study 9

A Living Sacrifice

Read Romans 12 and 13

Observation Questions

1. What does Paul say in Romans 12:3–8 are the gifts Christ gives to his body?

2. According to Romans 12:9–21, what are some characteristics that mark a Christian?

3. According to Romans 13:1–10, how should we relate to authority? What fulfills the law?

4. What does Paul say in Romans 13:11–14 is coming, and how should we live as we wait?

Interpretation

For eleven chapters, Paul has been explaining what we know to be true about God and ourselves—the condemned state of every human, no matter their background or conduct; the way of faith begun in Abraham and the promises made to him; our death and resurrection with Christ; our struggle with sin; life by the Spirit; the history and future of God's nation, Israel, and how that relates to us, the Gentiles. Paul now finally gives us the commands, the "what to do," the ethics of the Christian life.

Romans 12:1–2. Notice that Paul points to the mercy of God—not guilt, shame, pride, or fear—as reason to to live a life of obedience and sacrifice. Roman pagans at the time would have offered sacrifices to multiple gods, hoping to obtain mercy, but Christian believers understand that Jesus already made the atoning sacrifice. The mercy that motivated his sacrifice is what in turn motivates us.

The transformation and renewal of our minds that Paul commands only happens by Scripture and the Spirit working together to show us God's will. As we spend time in the Word, the Spirit transforms our minds. The word used here is *metamorpho*—the same word used of Jesus in the Transfiguration (Matthew 17:2). This is how God changes our minds and shows us his will.

Romans 12:3–8. We were not meant to be able to fulfill all of our needs by ourselves. On the contrary, we belong to each other and we each have different functions. Paul warns against pride; we are to think of ourselves soberly, or sanely, with wisdom. To think "according to the measure of faith that God has assigned" means to have an understanding of your spiritual gifts and to use them accordingly.

Romans 12:9–16. We are to be devoted to one another. In contrast to so much of what we read, hear, and see in our twenty-first century world, *yes*, we *are* responsible for one another (in the body of Christ). Instead of doing all we can to be sure we succeed in whatever area, our job is to try to make *others* succeed. It goes against our nature for sure, which is why Paul has to explain it.

Paul describes different gifts and how they are used to care for the body. Paul tells us that we must never stop caring about the practical needs of the saints. Do you know who among your brothers and sisters in the church may be in need? Are you paying attention to such things?

Paul's exhortation to practice hospitality, which literally means "love for stranger," is not just for those who happen to be good at it; it's a command. In the early church, what we would think of as hotels were often dangerous, seedy, promiscuous places. Hospitality within the church was vital in the spreading of the gospel.

We do not live detached lives in our own little worlds. We find joy in our brothers' and sisters' joy. We mourn their losses. We do not act like snobs, choosing only to invite the interesting or "cool" people to dinners, events, or gatherings.

Romans 12:17–21. Thus far Paul has been discussing life as a body—loving, serving, sharing, sacrificing. But what about life with our enemies? How do we treat those who mistreat us? We are called on to pursue peace. Retaliation and revenge are God's job, not ours. We love our enemies in order that our kindness might soften their hearts and lead them to repentance.

Remember that our enemies are not just some caricature of evil "out there." Sometimes your "enemy" is your mother-in-law, your child, your boss, even your life group leader, your husband, or your neighbor. Whomever it may be, your response must be the same: overcome evil with good. If we curse them back, take revenge, gossip about them, repay hurt for hurt, or punish with our silence or quiet rejection, then we have repaid evil for evil. If, however, we bless those who are cruel to us, leave the judgment to God, and serve the person who is unkind to us, we have overcome evil with good. None of this is possible, of course, without the work of the Spirit in our hearts. Not only are we saved by the grace of God and given new life by his Spirit; we also live day to day in obedience by that same grace, relying on the Spirit.

Romans 13:1–5. Paul has outlined our relationship to God, to one another, and to our enemies. But what about our relationship to the human authority under which we all live? Paul lived during a time in which so many brothers and sisters experienced persecution for their faith that he simply assumes persecution in their personal lives as he pens his letters. Paul's stance toward governing officials in general is shockingly respectful, given the context into which he is writing. After treating the topic of authority, Paul speaks more broadly of loving one another, and of our ultimate hope—the return of the perfect and gentle authority on the day of our Lord.

All authority is derived from God's authority. Even the authority that Satan wields has been given to him (Luke 4:6). This presents many with a conundrum. Does blame therefore fall to God for the Hitlers, Saddam Husseins, and Stalins of the world? No. God is not the author of evil. He does not tempt anyone to evil, but each is tempted and deceived by their own desire (James 1). So are Christians to obey all governments everywhere even when they overstep their bounds? What about corrupt or abusive authorities? Clearly, there is a line that cannot be crossed. Believers must submit and obey in all ways when they can, right up to the line of what the Bible lays out as righteous. From there on, we must operate in a state of civil disobedience. There are many examples of this in Scripture, one of the clearest being the Hebrew midwives who were commanded by Pharaoh to kill all firstborn boys (Exodus 1). The midwives feared God and let the babies live. Sometimes obedience to God means disobedience to earthbound authorities.

But let us not fall off the horse the other way. Some Christians have a tendency to become cynical and disrespectful of their local or national authorities. Paul uses the same word to describe leaders of the state (*diakonoi*) as he uses in other places to describe ministers of the church. This understanding deflates popular secular/sacred divisions of the world. There is no such division. All truth and all authority—indeed, all things—belong to God.

Romans 13:6–7. These are the things Paul lists as being owed to others, and specifically being owed to those in authority: taxes, money, respect, and honor. We owe our representative leaders honor. What does this mean for our attitudes toward them, the way we speak and write about them, our social media posts concerning them, and the way we teach our children about them? We can look at this in all places of authority, from the president to our school principals to our church elders and deacons to the police officer writing us a ticket. Authority is not the enemy but has been put into place by our Father for our good.

Romans 13:8–10. Paul shifts from talking about what we owe to those in authority, whether honor, respect, or money, to the one debt we will never finish paying off—love. We can never be said to have finished our work of loving while on this earth.

Romans 14:11–14. We know what to do, but where do we find the motivation to do it? This continuous unpaid debt of love, including self-sacrifice and honoring others above ourselves, is a foreign work to our flesh. We have talked about being motivated by the mercy of God and his faithfulness to us. But Paul also tells us we are to be motivated by the future. The end is coming, and there must be an urgency with which we live. While the world seems to go on in the monotony of death, sin, and brokenness, Paul reminds us that the end could be right around the corner—even Jesus does not know the day or the hour. We could be making dinner, doing the dishes, putting children to bed, fixing our hair, or driving to work when suddenly our Lord will descend. All of the things that plague us now—the hopelessness, the frustrations, the sickness, the disappointment—all will be done in an instant. The kingdom that we have been hoping for, waiting for, and investing in will be upon us. Our king will be back to reign in full and to receive and reward his children. It really is going to happen. And it could be today.

If this is true, if the end of the night is so close, we must wake up and put aside the things done in the night. We must take off our night clothes of drunkenness, sexual immorality, and disagreements that lead to discord, conflict, and jealousy. In place of these things, we must dress ourselves with Jesus, walking as children of light, ready for battle. Much of this battle happens in our own minds, where we decide moment to moment what is true, who we are, and what we choose to believe. According to Paul, we have a choice. We can choose to be preoccupied with how to fulfill our selfish desires, or we can be vigilant, choosing again and again, moment by moment, to return in our minds to the kingdom and to live in the light of the King that is coming.

Reflection Questions

5. God is working through his Spirit and his Word to transform your mind and show you his will. Paul even uses the same word, *metamorpho,* that was used of Jesus in the Transfiguration (Matthew 17:2). What is the process you experience when God, through his Spirit and his Word, changes how you think or view a particular situation? Can you give any examples?

6. In Romans 12:6–8, Paul lists several gifts Christ gives to his body. Which one do you have? What does that look like when you are expressing that gift?

7. As Christians we are called to enter into the joys and sorrows that our brothers and sisters are experiencing in their lives. What about this is hard for you? What would it look like for you to grow in this area?

8. Paul describes the call of the believer to submit to and respect government authorities because they are set up by God. What about this call feels hard or confusing for you? What about it feels comforting and logical?

9. Describe an instance this week where you felt like you loved your neighbor as yourself. On the other hand, describe an instance this week where you felt like you did not love your neighbor well. What do you want to ask the Spirit to help you with in this area?

Focus Verse

I appeal to you therefore, brothers, by the mercies of God, to present your bodies as a living sacrifice, holy and acceptable to God, which is your spiritual worship. Do not be conformed to this world, but be transformed by the renewal of your mind, that by testing you may discern what is the will of God, what is good, acceptable, and perfect.

Romans 12:1–2

Reflections, curiosities, frustrations:

Study 10

Loving the Family of God

Read Romans 14, 15, and 16

Observation Questions

1. In Romans 14:1–12, what does Paul say about how we should respond to our fellow believers in areas where we differ?

2. What does Paul say in Romans 14:13–23 about how believers are to think about their personal choices and how those choices may impact their brothers and sisters?

3. Summarize Romans 15:1–21 in a few sentences.

4. How many different believers does Paul address and thank at the end of his letter to Romans? What is he instructing the Romans to do for all these people?

Interpretation

Paul continues to write about the practical implications for the Christian life in light of the first eleven chapters of Romans. He begins with the idea that, without careful love for one another, secondary issues in the Christian life can become primary issues. We are not given liberty simply to make ourselves happy but to love our brothers and sisters.

Romans 14:1–4. The word "faith" here has the approximate meaning of "conscience." Paul is probably referring to the Jews who have converted to Christianity as "weak." At issue was the fact that for their entire lives before converting, most devout Jews would have conformed to strict dietary laws of the Old Testament, which forbade the eating of certain meats and other foods. These brothers and sisters did not feel the freedom in their consciences to eat these formerly forbidden foods, even though all foods were declared "clean" by Christ himself.

Paul gives us the ruling principle here: Don't judge your fellow believer or look down on them; don't quarrel over opinions. The issues are different in the American church, but they still have the potential to cause massive problems. The use of alcohol, the mode of baptism, the existence and use of charismatic gifts, the precise nature of heaven and hell, which TV shows to watch, how we use our money, whether or not we smoke, what we eat, if we exercise, the use of antidepressants and birth control—all of these are nonessential issues that tempt us to judge and condemn one another.

Romans 14:5–12. Paul is concerned much less with what people do on certain days and much more that they are convinced in their own mind and heart that what they are doing pleases God. Let them listen to their own consciences. Remember, the goal is not absolute agreement in all of these things; these are not the central aspects of the Christian faith.

We will all be judged eventually by the King himself, so it makes no sense to judge one another improperly now. What good does it do for me to judge my sister? In fact, it does no good but only harm. I am a false judge, without the wisdom or the authority to make any judgments of her. She is the servant of Jesus, bound to him, sure to answer to him for every decision she has made. She has no reason to explain herself or justify certain decisions to me.

Romans 14:13–23. Here is another principle given to us by Paul: Love limits its own liberty out of respect for the weak.[1] This may call for a measure of sacrifice. There is no reason to go parading around with our freedom, forcing it down the throat of every other believer. In fact, Paul goes so far as to tell the Romans to keep their mouths shut, keeping their opinions about whether or not to eat certain meats and about what holy days to celebrate to themselves. While we must reeducate our consciences in order to enjoy the full pleasure, fellowship, and freedom of the gospel, we must not violate our own conscience or cause others to violate theirs. We move along in the faith at different speeds, understanding the implications of our faith at different rates. We must trust God to handle this process in our brothers and sisters.

Romans 15:1–4. Paul continues his plea for unity, setting his sights on Jews and Gentiles accepting each other in a way that gives God glory. We should not strive to please ourselves but our neighbor. This is not the negative sense that we call "people pleasing"—putting other people's opinions above God's. This is putting others' needs and consciences ahead of ours to encourage them. Why? Because this is what Jesus did. Who would have ever had more freedom than him? And yet he submitted his freedom for love's sake.

Romans 15:5–13. Paul's prayer for the Romans is that the Jews and Gentiles (roughly the weak and the strong) may be unified. Our free acceptance of one another brings praise to God. Jesus himself became a servant to the Jews, always pursuing the lost sheep of Israel while here on earth. In this sense, Jesus limited himself, choosing a focus for his ministry in order to serve this little nation. God had made promises to the patriarchs; Jesus was a big part of fulfilling them. The apostles were the continuance of that. But Paul's calling was to the Gentiles. He offers us four Old Testament passages that show the increasing inclusion of the Gentiles in the worship and kingdom of God. Paul is saying that this was God's purpose all along, that all the nations, including the Gentiles, would be blessed.

Romans 15:14–21. Paul uses priestly language, assuring these believers that his motivation is to present the Gentiles as an acceptable offering to God. While he wants to challenge them in these places of submitting to one another, he also wants to encourage them that he sees the work of the Holy Spirit among them.

Paul could have gone on and on about what he had accomplished, starting countless churches, evangelizing cities, writing so many letters and training so many leaders, even financially supporting himself as a tentmaker. But instead, he speaks of what Christ had accomplished through him. When he writes of having "fulfilled the ministry of the gospel of Christ," he does not mean that he had preached the gospel to every single person in this large area but that he had been first in bringing the gospel to the cities of the area.

Romans 15:22–29. Paul's total trip would have been more than 3,000 miles. He knows he will need the help of the Roman church on his way—their money, their hospitality, their prayers. On the way to Rome (though it is not at all on the way to Rome), Paul is taking a gift to the poorer believers in Jerusalem. This would be a token of the way in which the Jews and Gentiles embraced one another in Christ. Paul has been laying the groundwork for the significance of this gift all through Romans. He wants to see the reconciling ministry of Jesus Christ publicly demonstrated. The Jews had been the source of the story of faith for the Gentiles, giving them life and salvation. The Gentiles, then, could share their worldly possessions with the poorer Jews in the city of Jerusalem.

Romans 15:30–33. Paul begs these brothers and sisters to pray. And we who live later in redemptive history know that the prayers of the saints resulted in Paul eventually going to Rome, and probably even then making it to Spain. Do we pray as if our prayers matter? Do we pray as these saints must have, believing that God hears and chooses to act as a result of our requests? Paul describes their prayers as striving with him. In a very real way, when we pray for the work of the kingdom and its expansion, we are striving with those who do it.

Romans 16:1–2. Paul stops his address to the church as a whole and greets individuals with whom he already has a personal relationship. Phoebe was apparently a fellow believer who was about to move to Rome, so Paul takes the opportunity to both use her as a carrier and to commend her to the Roman church.

Romans 16:3–16. How did Paul know all of these people, since we know that he had never before visited the church in Rome? It is possible that Paul knew many of these believers in other cities or had come across them in other contexts and that they had made their way to the great city. Trade and commerce were at their peak in Rome, attracting more and more people to the opportunities there. And since the Jews were being let back into the city after the death of Claudius, who had expelled them, many who had been forced to other places against their will may have finally been returning. Paul may have known these people before their return.

Romans 16:17–19. It seemed that we were done with exhortations and directions, that Paul was giving his final greetings. Why does he break into such an urgent warning? Paul loves the Roman church, though he's never been there. He has seen firsthand what bad teaching or bad theology can do to a church.

Though he has written them thoroughly about so many matters, a moment of anxiety seizes him as he thinks of the damage possible in this beloved church. Though we don't know the specific circumstances of which he speaks, we know the danger is enough to interrupt his train of thought, and possibly he even took the pen in his own hand and physically wrote this part of the letter himself. He warns the Romans about people who talk about the Lord but don't serve him. They manipulate and deceive. Paul does not mince words here; he simply tells the believers to get away from those people.[2]

Romans 16:20. Here is the entirety of Genesis 3 to Revelation in one sentence. Paul encourages his brothers and sisters by reminding them of the imminent destruction of our enemy. Paul seems to allude to Genesis 3:15, where God says that while Satan will bruise the offspring of Adam and Eve, he will finally be bruised or crushed himself. This is our hope, is it not? Satan is going to lose. All of his influence and evil plans to harm the children of God will come to an end, and he will be thrown into the lake of fire (Revelation 19:19–21).

Romans 16:25–27. In his final benediction, all praise goes to Jesus as Paul gives us one last insight into the character and ability of our King. Though spoken of in the Old Testament, God's plan for the multiethnic church was not fully understood until the first century AD. Paul's calling to evangelize the nations was a big part of that church becoming a reality. The letter he is writing is addressed to a church that clearly displays this mystery, as the church is composed of both Jews and Gentiles. God is able to widen his blessing from his little flock of Israel to the whole of the nations. God is able to establish these new Gentile believers and to walk them toward obedience as they learn the ways of the kingdom. God is able to establish and secure these multiethnic churches, even in the harsh religious climate of first-century Rome, where Christians could expect persecution. God is able to protect his church from being led astray by false teachers. All praise be to him who is able!

Reflection Questions

5. Paul talks about being mindful of those who are "weak in the faith" by not quarreling over opinions with them. What are some specific topics or areas that you struggle with getting into unnecessary quarrels with fellow believers about?

6. Paul is calling us to humble ourselves for fellow believers like Christ did for us. Does this bring to light any present relationship that you need to pray through and consider limiting your freedom in order to help that brother or sister thrive? Pray and ask the Spirit to enable you to love in this way.

7. Paul is calling for unity and love between Jewish and Gentile believers, which would result in the praise of God. What have you seen disunity cause among believers you are around? How have you seen unity of believers lead to the praise of God?

8. Which story of Paul's various ministry friends in Romans 16:3–16 stood out to you the most? Why?

9. The closing verses of Romans are a doxology, or praise to God. What are some specific lines from Romans 16:25–27 that you find comforting?

10. What are your main takeaways from studying the Book of Romans?

Focus verse

Now to him who is able to strengthen you according to my gospel and the preaching of Jesus Christ, according to the revelation of the mystery that was kept secret for long ages but has now been disclosed and through the prophetic writings has been made known to all nations, according to the command of the eternal God, to bring about the obedience of faith—to the only wise God be glory forevermore through Jesus Christ! Amen.

Romans 16:25–27

Reflections, curiosities, frustrations:

Acknowledgments

Chris: To Michael, the business consultant, idea-giver, consistent sounding board, and strategizer for At His Feet, thank you again and *still* for believing in me and us. Rebecca, thank you for jumping in and working to exhaustion just because you love us. Renae, you continue to impress and encourage me with your gifts. Thank you, thank you, thank you for your willingness to serve with us. Jennifer, your singing Voxes and prayers do more for the kingdom than you could know. Hopers, your willingness to be honest with me for the sake of both our friendship and our writing partnership is a gift to me. Dr. Ray Ray, thank you for always encouraging Hope and me to keep doing this.

Hope: Ray, thank you for always cheering us on and reminding me why we do it. To our team this year that has been so selfless and giving with their time and talents—Renae and Rebecca, we love you! Jen, you have been the actual best, walking us through all things At His Feet Studies and, more importantly, life. To Redeemer Lincoln: You guys were the reason this all started. You let us hand you the original, weekly copies of Romans before At His Feet even existed. So here Romans is again, all tweaked and reworked, but you guys are still so much of how this all happened in the first place.

Notes

Introduction: The History Behind the Pages of Romans

1. English translation taken from the edition produced by Lutheran Publishing House, Adelaide, 1966.

Study 3. Christ Died for Us: Romans 5

1. Quoted in Longman and Garland, *Expositor's Bible Commentary*, 98.

2. Stott, *Message of Romans*, 155.

Study 4. Dead to Sin and Alive to God: Romans 6–7

1. Stott, *Message of Romans*, 167.

2. Reformed theologians have come to refer to three specific uses of the moral law of God (the Ten Commandments and their application): (1) Civil use: The law restrains sin in the world. For example, "do not murder" is the law in most countries, enforced by different levels of punishment. This is an external law that holds back the rampant evil in the world. (2) Pedagogical, or instructional, use: The law reveals sin to us in all of its deceit and points us to Christ. For example, Jesus uses the commandment

"do not murder" to reveal the hatred in our heart. (3) Normative use: The law acts as a norm of conduct, guiding believers in a life of grateful obedience. For example, "do not murder" not only refers to avoiding the act of deliberately killing another person; it encompasses loving others as we wish to be loved.

Study 5. More Than Conquerors: Romans 8

1. Stott, *Message of Romans,* 238.

2. Ibid., 245.

Study 6. Not Human Will, but God's Choice: Romans 9

1. Stott, *Message of Romans,* 266.

2. Longman and Garland, *Expositor's Bible Commentary,* 154.

3. Ibid., 158.

4. Stott, *Message of Romans,* 276.

Study 7. Preach the Good News: Romans 10

1. Keller, *Romans,* study 17.

2. Longman and Garland, *Expositor's Bible Commentary,* 162.

Study 10. Loving the Family of God: Romans 14–16

1. Stott, *Message of Romans,* 365.

2. Ferguson, "Closing Remarks?"

Bibliography

Ferguson, Sinclair B. "Closing Remarks?" Sermon delivered at First Presbyterian Church, Columbia, SC, June 27, 2010. Audio available at http://www.sermo naudio.com/sermoninfo.asp?SID=39129549.

Keller, Tim. *Romans: A Study Course in the Gospel, Leaders Guide.* New York: Redeemer Presbyterian Church, 2003. Available as a PDF download at http://www.gospelinlife.com/romans-a-study-course-in-the-gospel-g roup-study-product.

Longman, Tremper, and David Garland. *The Expositor's Bible Commentary.* Vol. 11, *Romans–Galatians.* Grand Rapids, MI: Zondervan, 2011.

Stott, John. *The Message of Romans: God's Good News for the World.* Downers Grove, IL: IVP Academic, 2001.

The Story of At His Feet Studies

A few years ago, Hope started looking for materials for the women's fall Bible study at our church. While she found a great number of quality Bible studies, she had a hard time finding studies written for women by women who were reformed. She also had a tough time finding in-depth studies of the Scripture that didn't take a whole lot of time. In a moment of desperation, Hope asked Chris if she would be willing to co-write a study on Romans, convincing her by asking, "I mean, really, how hard could it be?" And so it began. Weekly emails back and forth, Chris deep in commentaries, Hope mulling over questions, tweaking, editing, asking, pondering. A group of women at Redeemer Presbyterian Church in Lincoln, Nebraska, patiently bore with us as we experimented with them every week and learned to find our rhythm as writers.

Two years later, Hope approached Chris again, softening her up by telling her she could choose any book she wanted: 1 Samuel it was. Old Testament narrative is the best. Another study was born. About this time, women started asking us for copies of the two studies we had written. While trying to send endless PDFs to people around the country via email, a pastor friend who happens to be a publisher approached Chris and Hope at a party, offering to publish the Bible studies. Suddenly, we had a way to get these into the hands of women who could use them. This had been the point of the whole enterprise--to help make the book of Romans accessible to women. But what would the name be?

During the first century, when Jesus walked the earth, a Jewish rabbi would have been surrounded by his students, with some of the men sitting at his feet to learn and listen. This was the custom, the understood norm of the day. But in Luke 10:39, *Mary* sat at the feet of Jesus. Mary, a woman, was taught by this unconventional rabbi. Mary was given the dignity of taking in his words, his pauses, his tone. To Jesus, she was every bit as worthy of his teaching as the men in the room were—and so are we, his women students today. And so we are At His Feet Bible Studies, hoping to sit at the feet of Jesus while we study his Word.

Other At His Feet Studies

We pray that you will continue to sit at the feet of Jesus, studying his Word. To help you with this, we have also written Bible studies on these books of the Bible:

1 Samuel (16 studies)

Philippians (12 studies)

Psalms (13 studies)

Luke: Part 1 (13 studies)

Luke: Part 2 (14 studies)

Luke: Part 3 (12 studies)

The Servant King: A Study of the Gospel of Luke (10 studies)

Galatians (8 studies)

Gálatas (en español, 8 estudios)

Lamentations (7 studies)

Colossians (10 studies)

You can find all of our studies at athisfeetstudies.com.